by Tammy Gagne

Consultant: Dr. Jackie Gai, DVM

raintree
a Capstone company — publishers for children

Raintree is an imprint of Capstone Global Library Limited, a company incorporated in England and Wales having its registered office at 264 Banbury Road, Oxford, OX2 7DY – Registered company number: 6695582

www.raintree.co.uk
myorders@raintree.co.uk

## Editorial Credits

Carrie Braulick Sheely, editor; Sarah Bennett and Juliette Peters, designers; Tracy Cummins, media researcher; Tori Abraham, production specialist

ISBN 9781474712040 (hardback)
20 19 18 17 16
10 9 8 7 6 5 4 3 2 1

ISBN 9781474712064 (paperback)
21 20 19 18 17
10 9 8 7 6 5 4 3 2 1

## British Library Cataloguing in Publication Data

A full catalogue record for this book is available from the British Library.

## Acknowledgements

We would like to thank the following for permission to reproduce photographs:
FLPA: Lacz, 6 Bottom; Getty Images: Per-Gunnar Ostby, 11; iStockphoto: Angelika Stern, 8, mit4711, 19, WLDavies, 13; Minden Pictures: Anup Shah, 5; Shutterstock: Albie Venter, 12, Anan Kaewkhammul, 6 Middle Left, bonga1965, 18, EcoPrint, 6 Middle Right, Erwin Niemand, 15, gualtiero boffi, 6 Top, Johan Swanepoel, 17, Nachaliti, Cover, Peter Schwarz, 9, rujithai, 3, Stacey Ann Alberts, 2, Sue Berry, Cover Back, Tamer Desouky, 1; SuperStock: Biosphoto, 21; Thinkstock: Anup Shah, 14

Every effort has been made to contact copyright holders of material reproduced in this book. Any omissions will be rectified in subsequent printings if notice is given to the publisher.

Printed and bound in the United Kingdom.

# CONTENTS

# STRENGTH IN NUMBERS

Hyenas aren't the biggest animals in Africa. The largest hyenas are only about 0.8 metres (2.5 feet) tall. But don't let their size fool you. These animals are powerful **predators**. A group of spotted hyenas can take down animals three times their own size.

## FACT

Spotted hyenas work together when hunting **herd** animals, such as zebras. These hyenas usually hunt in groups of three to five. But they may form larger groups.

**predator** an animal that hunts other animals for food

**herd** a large group of animals that lives or moves together

# PREDATORS WITH A PLAN

Hyenas usually attack a young or weak member of a herd. One hyena rushes into the group to **distract** the other animals. The remaining hyenas work on cutting the target off from the herd. Once they have the **prey** alone, the hyenas attack. After a kill is made, hyenas often fight over the **carcass**.

spotted hyena

striped hyena

**distract** to draw attention away from something

**prey** an animal hunted by another animal for food

**carcass** the body of a dead animal

**species** a group of animals with similar features

# HYENA SPECIES

There are four hyena **species**. They include the spotted hyena, striped hyena and brown hyena. The aardwolf is also a member of the hyena family. However, its hunting habits and diet are very different from those of the other species.

brown hyena

aardwolf

| Species | Hunting Habits | What It Eats | Where It Lives |
|---|---|---|---|
| Spotted Hyena | alone or in groups | wildebeest, zebras, antelope, gazelles, lizards, rabbits, foxes, birds, warthogs, sheep, goats, animals already dead | Africa |
| Striped Hyena | mainly alone | birds, lizards, rabbits, sheep, goats, insects, fruit, animals already dead | Africa, Asia |
| Brown Hyena | alone or in small groups | birds, rodents, lizards, insects, fruit, eggs, animals already dead | Africa |
| Aardwolf | alone | mainly termites | Africa |

# WHATEVER IT TAKES

Spotted hyenas are the largest hyena species. They kill at least three-quarters of their own food. These hyenas hunt wildebeest, zebras, gazelles and warthogs. Other species eat smaller animals, such as mice, rabbits and even bugs.

Hyenas are also **scavengers**. They eat meat other predators have left behind.

## FACT

Hyenas sometimes try to steal the kills of lions. But in western Africa, lions have been seen eating the kills of hyenas. Prey can be hard to find in the area.

**scavenger** an animal that feeds on animals that are already dead

# OUTRUNNING PREY

Hyenas use their speed and **stamina** to hunt. When racing after zebras and other fast prey, spotted hyenas can run up to 60 kilometres (37 miles) per hour. They can keep running for up to 5 km (3 mi) at 40 to 50 km (25 to 31 mi) per hour.

**stamina** the ability to keep doing an activity for long periods of time

# CRUSHING JAWS

Hyenas use their sharp teeth and powerful jaws to kill prey. A spotted hyena's bite is as strong as a lion's. Most predators only eat the meat from their kills. But hyenas eat the bones, teeth and even hooves of their prey!

## FACT

Hyenas can **digest** the bones and teeth of the animals they eat. But a hyena will often throw up any hooves or horns it eats.

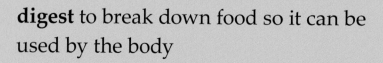

**digest** to break down food so it can be used by the body

# SHARP SENSES

Hyenas hunt at night. They depend on their sharp eyesight and hearing to find prey in the dark. But it's their sense of smell that sets hyenas apart from most other African predators. Their noses can pick up the scent of a carcass up to 4 km (2.5 mi) away.

## FACT

Hyenas also find carcasses by watching for **vultures** flying overhead. The hyenas then follow the birds to the food.

**vulture** a large bird that eats dead animals and has a featherless head

14

# ONE ON ONE

Spotted hyenas usually hunt in groups. Brown and striped hyenas often hunt small animals alone. But spotted hyenas can take down big animals on their own. One spotted hyena can easily take down a lone springbok. This African gazelle can weigh nearly as much as the hyena.

## FACT

Hyenas are related to cats. But they do not **stalk** prey like cats do. Instead, hyenas depend on their speed to outrun the animals.

**stalk** to hunt slowly and quietly

A brown hyena carries off its prey.

# MEALS ON THE RUN

Hyenas defend their kills from other predators. But they seem to know when the odds are against them. When hyenas are losing the fight, they will run away. But before they do, they often tear a large chunk of meat off the kill.

## FACT
Spotted hyenas make more than 11 different sounds.

# MINE!

As many as 80 hyenas may live in groups called clans. In these clans, hyenas have a social rank. The leaders eat first. Other members may have to fight to get part of a kill.

Spotted hyenas are not in danger of dying out. But numbers of other hyena species are declining. People continue to watch hyenas' numbers. The predators are an important part of African **ecosystems**.

# AMAZING BUT TRUE!

Because hyenas don't always eat every day, they may **gorge** themselves when they make a large kill. A single hyena can eat 15 kilogrammes (33 pounds) of meat at one feeding. That's like a person eating about 132 quarter-pound hamburgers in a single sitting!

**ecosystem** a group of animals and plants that work together with their surroundings

**gorge** to eat greedily

# GLOSSARY

**carcass** the dead body of an animal

**digest** to break down food so it can be used by the body

**distract** to draw attention away from something

**ecosystem** a group of animals and plants that work together with their surroundings

**gorge** to eat greedily

**herd** a large group of animals that lives or moves together

**predator** an animal that hunts other animals for food

**prey** an animal hunted by another animal for food

**scavenger** an animal that feeds on animals that are already dead

**species** a group of animals with similar features

**stalk** to hunt slowly and quietly

**stamina** the ability to keep doing an activity for long periods of time

**vulture** a large bird that eats dead animals and has a featherless head

# READ MORE

*Hunting with Hyenas* (When Animals Attack!), Kennon O'Mara (Gareth Stevens Pub., 2014).

*Hyenas* (Ferocious Fighting Animals), Julia J. Quinlan (PowerKids Press, 2013).

*Hyenas* (Blastoff!), Kari Schuetz (Bellwether Media, 2012).

# WEBSITES

**African Wildlife Foundation: Hyena**
https://www.awf.org/wildlife-conservation/hyena

**BBC Earth: The Truth About Spotted Hyenas**
http://www.bbc.com/earth/story/20141028-the-truth-about-spotted-hyenas

**National Geographic Kids: Spotted Hyena**
http://kids.nationalgeographic.com/animals/spotted-hyena/.

# COMPREHENSION QUESTIONS

1. Look at the chart on page 7. Explain one way the hyena species are different from one another. Explain one way they are the same.

2. Name a sense hyenas have and explain how it helps them hunt.

# INDEX